Cocktails & Mi

> Authors: Tanja Dusy | Alessandra Redies

Contents

Fundamentals

The Recipes

Appendix

Mix it, Baby!

How about a small aperitif before dinner, or perhaps a few dazzling tropical drinks for your next party? Mixing cocktails yourself is the latest trend; it's fun and very easy. All you need is a few basic bar utensils and some basic types of alcohol, and you're ready to go! Supplement these with the right recipes for cocktails both old and new, and you've brought the trendy bar scene into your home. Enjoy happy hour every day, and not just for an hour!

The Home Cocktail Party

1 | Selecting recipes

Who likes to drink cocktails alone? Accompanied by good friends, they just taste better. And even more so if you've made the right preparations, starting with your selection of recipes: two to three different-flavored drinks, plus one non-alcoholic drink will do. Don't pick too many recipes, otherwise, you'll get lost in a forest of bottles while each guest asks to try a different drink. Also, select some drinks that you can prepare before your guests arrive. Something like a Caipirinha or Mint Julep is always a good choice because you can crush

1 *You can easily prepare limes and mint in the glass.*

the limes and mint with sugar before you need them, cover, and set aside.

Tip: A useful gadget to have for happy hour is a blender. With it, you can easily make drinks for a group using crushed ice.

2 | Ice cubes

Whether shaken or stirred, ice cubes are an essential ingredient in successful cocktails. They should be as fresh as possible so that the drinks won't take on the flavor of the food in your freezer. The second rule of ice cubes for cocktail parties: You'll need a lot of ice cubes for blending, about seven or more per drink. The easiest thing to do is to buy bags at the store. These are especially practical because you don't run the risk of things falling into your ice cube trays while they freeze!

3 | Snacks, etc.

To keep the alcohol from going straight to your head, be sure to serve cocktail snacks. You'll find a small and delicious assortment on page 13. For your information: Dairy products such as hard cheeses and spreads inhibit alcohol absorption, helping to prevent headaches the morning after. For example, you can include crackers with cheese spreads or the cheese platter from page 13 in your assortment of snacks.

Also, be sure to keep plenty of water on hand so that the cocktails aren't used to quench thirst.

Shaking Cocktails Right

It isn't hard to shake like a pro, and it makes a big impression. All you need is a cocktail shaker, preferably one made of stainless steel with a built-in strainer. For shakers without an integral strainer (for example, a Boston shaker), you'll also need a bar strainer. Add to this a lot of thoroughly frozen ice, a little muscle power and relaxed wrists, and you have all the elements used by a professional barkeeper. To get an idea, try making this Aperol Sour.

Aperol Sour

MAKES 1 DRINK

- ¼ cup Aperol
- ⅛ cup plus 2 tsp freshly squeezed lemon juice
- 2 tsp sugar syrup (i.e. simple syrup)

TIP

Making your own sugar syrup (or also called simply syrup)

Brink 4¼ cups water to a full boil and stir in 4⅓ cups granulated sugar. Stir constantly until the sugar has dissolved and the liquid is clear. Let simmer for a little while longer— the longer it simmers, the thicker the syrup. Let cool completely and transfer to a bottle with a tight seal.

1 Gather together Aperol, lemon juice, sugar syrup, a cocktail shaker, and a jigger.

2 Using the jigger, carefully measure out the liquids into the shaker along with 4 ice cubes. Cover.

3 Shake the shaker vigorously up and down for about 20 seconds, until condensation forms on the outside.

4 Strain the shaker contents through the integral strainer or a bar strainer into a 5–6 ounce glass containing 3 ice cubes.

A variety of glasses

Martini or cocktail glass (4 ounce):
Used for cocktails that are served straight up and therefore best accommodated in a stemmed glass—it allows you to hold onto the stem so you don't warm the drink with your hand.

Collins glass (8 ounce):
Just about everybody keeps ordinary tall glasses in their cupboard, which makes them the best choice for endless mixing fun. Gin & Tonic, Horse's Neck, etc., are especially stylish when served in a collins glass.

Large cocktail glass (10 ounce):
Many tropical cocktails involve a lot of liquid; a large cocktail glass gives them the space they need. You can use either a special, fancy glass or an ordinary drinking glass.

Rocks glass or Old Fashioned glass (5–6 ounce):
With its heavy base, this glass is traditionally used for drinking pure spirits on the rocks. A Caipirinha is a drink well-suited to a rocks glass.

Liqueur glass (2–3 ounce):
Aperitifs are served in small amounts; otherwise it defeats their purpose, which is to stimulate the appetite before a meal. They require medium-height glasses that have a heavy base and are slightly wider at the top.

Champagne glass (2–3 ounce):
Regardless of whether you use a saucer, goblet or flute, all are suitable glasses for sparkling wine and champagne cocktails. Again, what matters is the stem, which allows you to serve a Bellini, for example, without adding ice.

Equipment for shaking and stirring

Jigger: Shaking cocktails isn't hard, but you have to have a jigger! Measuring ingredients by sight results in some awful-tasting drinks. That's why you need a double jigger with a 1–2 ounce shot glass.

Cocktail shaker: A shaker is also part of your basic equipment. The standard model has three pieces: a base for the ingredients, an insert with an integral strainer, and a small cap that you can remove to pour.

Mixing glass: Anything that isn't shaken or prepared directly in the glass is stirred in a mixing glass to preserve the purity and strength of the spirits. You can use either a tall glass with a pour spout or the base of the shaker.

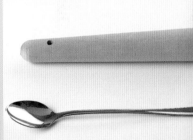

Bar strainer: You don't usually need a strainer. Most cocktail shakers have an integral strainer (except a Boston strainer) through which the drink is poured, and many mixing glasses have a pour spout that holds back the ice.

Ice crusher: A good-quality ice crusher is worth the price. A cheap one won't last long, so rather than buying an inexpensive model, you can also try wrapping ice in a kitchen towel and pounding it with a wooden mallet.

Muddler and bar spoon: To squeeze out limes, use a muddler or, in a pinch, use the back of a spoon. A long-handled bar spoon is good for stirring drinks in the mixing glass.

Some commonly used spirits

Vodka & bourbon:
Due to continuous distillation, the Russian "little water" has an almost neutral flavor. Usually distilled from grain, this clear spirit goes with almost all hard liquors and juices and is also delicious straight and ice cold. Bourbon, a distillate from a fermented mash of corn and other grains, must be stored in charred oak barrels for at least two years before bottling. Afterwards, it blends well with sour and bitter flavors such as lemon, vermouth, ginger ale, and mint.

Rum and cachaça:
Whether white, gold, or dark, all rum is produced by fermenting and distilling sugar cane juice. Dark rum is tinted by adding caramel. In contrast, cachaça, the national drink of Brazil, is distilled from raw sugar cane and is always clear. Good-quality cachaça is also delicious straight. Made famous in Europe through its use in the Caipirinha, cachaça is also the basis for Batidas, which contain cachaça, fruit juices, sugar, and crushed ice. All types of rum can be used in tropical drinks.

Tequila: This Mexican distillate is derived from the agave plant. White tequila is bottled shortly after distillation. Gold tequila is aged in oak barrels for up to four years, giving it a smoky flavor. Tequila is traditionally drunk straight: A pinch of salt is placed on the web of skin between the thumb and forefinger. The drinker licks the salt, downs a hearty shot of tequila, and then bites into a piece of lime. Tequila is also ideal for mixing, and is one of the few spirits that blends well with cachaça.

Gin: This clear spirit made from pure alcohol, juniper berries, and many additional herbs and spices—including, for example, anise, cardamom, caraway, and cinnamon—took the world by storm in the 1920s and 30s in the form of the ever popular Gin & Tonic. Generally, gin goes better in bitter and sour drink creations. Besides mixing well with tonic water, it's delicious with lemon, vermouth, Angostura, or curaçao triple sec. It can be labeled "Dry Gin" only if it was produced without added sugar.

Spanish brandy & cognac: Both these brandies are based on wine. Traditionally, this famous Spaniard comes from Jerez de la Frontera. Cognac, on the other hand, can wear its name only if it comes from the French region of Charente and can be bottled only after aging for at least 24 months in oak barrels. Sherry and cognac blend well with rum, cream, cocoa, or orange liqueur. Another specialty brandy from Chile is the finely aromatic pisco, distilled from a wine made with Muscat grapes.

Bitter aperitifs: The most famous are two Italians: Campari, the brilliant red herbal liqueur, and Aperol, which is made from a blend of rhubarb, herbs, alcohol, and other ingredients. Their fame is due, in large part, to their low alcohol content, which ranges from 25% vol (Campari) to 11% vol (Aperol). In addition, when mixed with club soda, tonic water or fruit juices, they make a quick, refreshing long drink fit for all occasions. Sparkling wine and champagne also go well with the flavor components of both these bitter aperitifs.

Vermouth: Vermouth is a wine aperitif distilled with herbs and spices. There are three types: fruity dry vermouth, the slightly vanilla-flavored vermouth bianco, and the bittersweet, caramel-colored vermouth rosso. Their flavor is an excellent complement to gin or vodka, but you can also drink them straight on the rocks.

Anises: Whether Pernod, pastis, ouzo, or the recently re-legalized absinthe, all have a very distinct anise flavor that makes them somewhat difficult to mix. In its Greek homeland, ouzo is usually drunk straight. Pastis, Pernod, and absinthe are diluted with water or fruit juice at a ratio of 1:5. Pastis and Pernod also go well with orange (juice or liqueur) and cream. Use anises sparingly, because the anise flavor can easily overwhelm everything else.

Some commonly used liqueurs

Orange liqueurs: The most famous and strongest (40% vol alcohol) has got to be Cointreau, and the most striking is blue curaçao. Triple sec has a similar flavor. They all blend well with orange juice and strong spirits such as vodka, rum, and gin.

Bailey's Irish Cream: It was the first of its kind and with its mixture of cream, Irish whiskey, and chocolate, it is still the most popular cream liqueur. You can drink it on the rocks or, even better, with brandy, vodka, or in a cream combination.

Cream liqueurs: Sweetened liqueurs such as crème de menthe, crème de cacao, and crème de cassis serve to color and sweeten your cocktails. As a rule, mix fruit liqueurs with their corresponding juice (for example, cassis with black currant nectar).

Herbal liqueurs: These are strong and very spicy, so measure them out carefully! Galliano has a hint of vanilla, while Bénédictine and Chartreuse are extremely spicy. Use the bitter Angostura only one drop at a time.

Fruit Brandies: Cherry and apricot brandy are made from a brandy base, plus fermented fruit juice. They mix well with cream liqueurs or fruit juices.

Amaretto and coconut liqueur: With its fine almond aroma amaretto, the Italian classic, softens hard liquors and refines creamy cocktails. Coconut liqueurs are relative newcomers to the bar scene and go well with all tropical spirits, especially rum.

Garnishing like a pro

Paper umbrellas, etc.: For nostalgic types, these will evoke the ambiance of a tropical bar. You'll find packages of colorful garnishing sets in the housewares department of any large store.

Salted and sugared rims: Dip the rim of the glass in lemon juice or, to give it color, in colorful syrups or liqueurs. Then dip it into a dish of salt or sugar and gently knock off the excess.

Fruit skewers: Take chunks of ripe, but firm fruit that matches the color and flavor of your cocktail and thread them onto a cocktail skewer (for example, pineapple, grapes, and kiwi). Lay the skewer across the rim of the glass.

Twists and leaves: Take a thin, spiral twist of peel from a lemon, lime, or orange and hang it on the rim of the glass, or place fresh sprigs or mint or lemon balm in the finished cocktail.

Syrup swirls: Colorful syrups and liqueurs drizzled carefully into the glass along the sides look especially nice in creamy cocktails.

Colorful ice cubes: These are fantastic in fruity cocktails. Make ice cubes from fruit juices (for example, orange juice or cherry nectar). Ice cubes in which berries or pieces of fruit have been frozen are especially attractive in clear drinks.

11

Non-alcoholic cocktails

Caribbean Cooler: Combine ¼ cup freshly squeezed orange juice, ¼ cup pineapple juice, ¼ cup peach nectar, 4 teaspoons cherry juice, ⅛ cup freshly squeezed lime juice, 4 teaspoons cream of coconut, and 1 dash grenadine with 4 ice cubes and shake for about 20 seconds.

Dragon's Blood: Combine ⅓ cup ice-cold red fruit tea, ¼ cup blood orange nectar, 4 teaspoons lime juice, 2 teaspoons cream of coconut, and 2 teaspoons almond syrup and stir well. Pour into a collins glass with 4 slices of lime and 4 ice cubes.

Orange Delight: Combine ¼ cup each of peeled, finely diced canta-loupe, papaya, and mango with ⅓ cup freshly squeezed orange juice, ⅓ cup passion fruit nectar, 4 teaspoons freshly squeezed lemon juice, 4 tea spoons almond syrup, and 3 ice cubes and purée in a blender.

Golden Autumn: Finely dice 1 piece candied ginger in syrup and place 1 teaspoon clear pear juice and 1 teaspoon white grape juice and stir. Top up with ginger ale.

Rosamunde: Combine ¼ cup blood orange juice, ⅛ cup strawberry syrup, ⅛ cup cream, 4 teaspoons freshly squeezed lemon juice, 1 fresh egg yolk, and 4 ice cubes and shake for about 20 seconds. Then strain into a martini glass.

Mimi Shake: Combine ⅔ cup well-chilled milk and 3 table-spoons mint syrup and stir. Pour into a cocktail glass and add 1–2 scoops chocolate chip ice cream.

Cocktail snacks

Cheese Rounds

5 dried apricots
⅓ cup Grappa (optional)
½ lb fresh goat cheese
½ tbs finely chopped
fresh rosemary
Salt
Pepper
20 pumpernickel rounds
3 tbs chopped pistachios

Dice apricots very finely
and soak overnight in
Grappa. Mix well with
goat cheese and
rosemary and carefully
season to taste with salt
and pepper. Spread
cheese mixture evenly
onto pumpernickel
rounds and sprinkle
with pistachios.

Summer Pinwheels

1–2 pkg frozen puff
pastry dough (10½ oz)
¼ cup dried tomatoes
in oil
¼ cup black olives in oil
½ cup walnuts
1 tsp herbes de Provence
2 tbs freshly grated
Parmesan
1 egg yolk
1 tbs milk

Thaw puff pastry dough.
Finely chop tomatoes,
olives, and walnuts. Stir in
herbs and Parmesan. Roll
out dough on a floured
work surface. Spread with
the mixture and roll up
lengthwise. Cut into ⅓
inch slices and place on
a baking sheet lined with
parchment paper. Whisk
egg yolk and milk, brush
onto pinwheels, and bake
in an oven preheated to
375°F (middle rack) for
10–12 minutes.

Curry Shards

3 red onions
2 tbs olive oil
1 round store-bought
pizza dough (about 8 oz;
in the refrigerated section)
2 tbs chopped
fresh parsley
⅔ cup sour cream
1 tsp curry powder
Salt

Peel onions, cut into
rings, and braise in hot
oil. Place pizza dough on
a backing sheet lined with
parchment paper. Stir
parsley into sour cream,
season to taste with curry
and salt, and spread onto
dough. Top with onions.
Bake in an oven preheat-
ed to 425°F (middle rack)
for about 15 minutes until
crispy. Cut into small
pieces and serve warm.

Chicken on Chips

¾ lb chicken fillet
1 small can pineapple
chunks (reserve juice)
2 tbs oil
Salt
Pepper
1 clove garlic
3 tbs soy sauce
½ tsp Sambal Oelek
2 tbs chopped fresh
cilantro
1 bag chili tortilla chips

Dice chicken. Drain pine-
apple in a strainer, saving
the juice. Brown chicken in
hot oil and season with salt
and pepper. Peel garlic,
squeeze through a press,
and add. Add soy sauce and
7 tablespoons pineapple
juice. Bring to a boil and
remove from heat. Stir in
Sambal Oelek and cilantro.
Let stand for 3 hours. Place
1 piece of chicken and 1
piece of pineapple on
each tortilla chip.

Sour & Aromatic

Lemon, lime, and grapefruit give many cocktails their kick. Combine them with bitter, aromatic spirits such as vermouth, bitters or herbal liqueurs, and their goodness gets even better!

Greek Cocktail

MAKES 1 DRINK

- ➤ 1½ tbs ouzo
  2 tbs grenadine syrup
  3 thin slices lime
  Club soda for topping up
- ➤ Plus:
  Ice cubes
  Cocktail shaker
  Bar strainer
  Collins glass (8 oz)

1 | Combine ouzo, grenadine and 4 ice cubes in the shaker, close, and shake vigorously for about 20 seconds.

2 | Place lime slices and 4-5 ice cubes in the collins glass. Strain shaker contents into the glass. Top up with club soda.

Double Apple Smash

MAKES 1 DRINK

- ➤ 10–15 fresh mint leaves
  1 tbs sugar syrup (i.e. simple sugar)
  ⅛ cup plus 2 tsp Calvados
  ¼ cup unfiltered apple juice
  1 dash freshly squeezed lemon juice
- ➤ Plus:
  Crushed ice
  Muddler
  Collins glass (8 oz)

1 | Rinse mint under cold water, pat dry, and place in the collins glass. Pour sugar syrup on top and crush mint slightly with the muddler.

2 | Fill glass with crushed ice. Pour on Calvados, apple juice, and lemon juice. Stir once and serve with a straw.

15

Classic
Martini

MAKES 1 DRINK

➤ ⅓ cup gin
1½ tbs dry vermouth
(e.g. Martini Extra Dry)
1 large green olive
(in brine)
➤ Plus:
Ice cubes
Mixing glass
Bar strainer
Martini glass (4 oz)

1 | In the mixing glass,
combine gin, vermouth,
and 8–10 ice cubes and
stir vigorously for about
6 seconds.

2 | Strain into the martini
glass. Carefully place the olive
in the glass. Serve immediately.

TIP For a slightly acidic
flavor, squeeze 1 piece
lemon peel over the
drink so that the
essential oils drip into
the glass, then drop
the peel in the glass.

Refreshing
Gin Fizz

MAKES 1 DRINK

➤ ¼ cup gin
⅛ cup plus 2 tsp freshly
squeezed lemon juice
1½ tbs sugar syrup
(i.e. simple syrup)
1 tsp sugar
1 dash club soda
➤ Plus:
Ice cubes
Cocktail shaker
Bar strainer
Collins glass (8 oz)

1 | Combine gin, lemon juice,
sugar syrup, sugar and 4 ice
cubes in the shaker, close, and
shake vigorously for about
20 seconds.

2 | Strain into the collins glass
over 3–4 ice cubes. Top up
with club soda.

➤ Variations: If you want to
take this drink in a different
flavor direction, replace
the gin with white rum,
bourbon, whiskey,
or vodka.

Short Drink
Gimlet

MAKES 1 DRINK

➤ ¼ cup gin
⅛ cup plus 2 tsp Rose's
Lime Juice
➤ Plus:
Ice cubes
Mixing glass
Bar strainer
Martini glass (4 oz)

1 | In the mixing glass, com-
bine gin, lime juice, and 4 ice
cubes and stir vigorously for
about 8 seconds.

2 | Strain into the martini glass.

TIP Here's a great base for
non-alcoholic cocktails:
Lemon-Grass Grape
Juice. Finely chop 1
lemon grass stalk. Place
in 1 cup white grape
juice, bring to a boil,
and let stand overnight.
Pour through a strainer
and use! For example,
combine ¼ cup lemon-
grass grape juice, 2 tea-
spoons lime juice, and 1
dash non-alcoholic bit-
ters, stir, and pour into
a glass with 3 ice cubes.

Classic
Singapore Sling

MAKES 1 DRINK

➤ ¼ cup gin
⅛ cup plus 2 tsp freshly squeezed lemon juice
1½ tbs sugar syrup (i.e. simple syrup)
Club soda for topping up
1½ tbs cherry brandy
➤ Plus:
Ice cubes
Cocktail shaker
Bar strainer
Collins glass (8 oz)
2 straws

1 | Combine gin, lemon juice, sugar syrup, and 4 ice cubes in the shaker. Close and shake vigorously for about 20 seconds. Strain shaker contents into the collins glass over 3 ice cubes.

2 | Pour a little club soda into the shaker, swirl it around briefly, and then strain it into the drink. Drizzle cherry brandy over the top. Serve with the straws.

Sour | Strong
Jerez Sling

MAKES 1 DRINK

➤ ¼ cup brandy (e.g. Veterano)
⅛ cup plus 2 tsp freshly squeezed lemon juice
1½ tbs grenadine syrup
Club soda for topping up
1 tbs blue curaçao
➤ Plus:
Ice cubes
Cocktail shaker
Bar strainer
Collins glass (8 oz)
2 straws

1 | Combine brandy, lemon juice, grenadine, and 4 ice cubes in the shaker. Place top on shaker to close and shake vigorously for about 20 seconds. Strain shaker contents into the collins glass over 3 ice cubes.

2 | Pour a little club soda into the shaker, swirl it around briefly, and then strain it into the drink. Drizzle blue curaçao over the top. Serve with the straws.

Classic Aperitif
Americano

MAKES 1 DRINK

➤ ⅛ cup Campari
⅛ cup vermouth rosso (e.g. Martini Rosso)
2–4 tsp club soda
1 piece orange peel
➤ Plus:
Ice cubes
Liqueur glass (2–3 oz)

1 | Place 3 ice cubes in the liqueur glass and pour on Campari and vermouth. Top up with club soda.

2 | Squeeze orange peel over the drink so that the essential oils drip into the glass.

➤ Variation: Use a larger glass (5 oz) and add ⅛ cup gin to the ingredients to make a **Negroni,** another classic aperitif.

Tart and Sweet
Limerol

MAKES 1 DRINK

➤ ½ lime
2 tsp brown sugar
⅛ lb watermelon
¼ cup Aperol
Ice-cold, dry sparkling wine for topping up
➤ Plus:
Crushed ice
Muddler
Blender
Collins glass (8 oz)
1 straw

1 | Rinse lime under hot water, cut into small pieces, and place in the collins glass. Sprinkle sugar on top and crush lime thoroughly with the muddler.

2 | Remove seeds from watermelon and dice finely. Place Aperol and watermelon in the blender and blend until the melon is completely puréed.

3 | Fill collins glass about ⅓ full with crushed ice. Pour on melon mixture and stir well. Top up with sparkling wine and serve with the straw.

Summery
Sour Peach

MAKES 1 DRINK

➤ ⅛ cup plus 2 tsp white rum
2 tsp maraschino
1½ tbs Aperol
1½ tbs freshly squeezed lemon juice
⅓ cup peach nectar
1 dash strawberry syrup
➤ Plus:
Ice cubes
Cocktail shaker
Bar strainer
Collins glass (8 oz)
1 straw

1 | Combine rum, maraschino, Aperol, lemon juice, peach nectar, strawberry syrup, and 4 ice cubes in the shaker. Place top on the shaker and shake vigorously for about 20 seconds.

2 | Strain shaker contents into the collins glass over 3 ice cubes. Serve with the straw.

Bitter and Sour
Campari Citrus

MAKES 1 DRINK

➤ 1 lime
⅛ plus 2 tsp Campari
½ cup orange juice
⅓ cup freshly squeezed pink grapefruit juice
➤ Plus:
Ice cubes
Cocktail shaker
Bar strainer
Collins glass (8 oz)
1 straw

1 | Rinse lime under hot water, wipe dry, cut in half crosswise, and cut into eighths lengthwise. Place lime pieces and lime juice in the collins glass.

2 | Combine Campari, orange juice, grapefruit juice, and 3 ice cubes in the shaker. Place top on the shaker and shake vigorously for about 20 seconds.

3 | Strain shaker contents into the collins glass and serve with the straw.

Refreshing | Aromatic
Frothy Apple

MAKES 1 DRINK

➤ ⅛ cup Calvados

¼ cup unfiltered apple juice

2 tsp freshly squeezed lemon juice

1½ tbs cherry syrup

1 fresh egg white (optional)

➤ Plus:

Ice cubes

Cocktail shaker

Bar strainer

Collins glass (8 oz)

1 straw

1 | Combine Calvados, apple juice, lemon juice, 2 teaspoons cherry syrup, egg white and 4 ice cubes in the shaker, close, and shake vigorously for about 20 seconds.

2 | Strain shaker contents into the collins glass over 3 ice cubes. Drizzle remaining 2 teaspoons cherry juice over the top and serve with the straw.

TIP The frothy head is created by the egg white, although you can also leave it out, if desired.

Strong | Foamy
Frothy Gin

MAKES 1 DRINK

➤ ⅛ cup gin

⅛ cup vermouth rosso (e.g. Martini Rosso)

2 tsp freshly squeezed lemon juice

1½ tbs grenadine syrup

1 fresh egg white

➤ Plus:

Ice cubes

Cocktail shaker

Bar strainer

Collins glass (8 oz)

1 straw

1 | Combine gin, vermouth, lemon juice, grenadine, egg white and 4 ice cubes in the shaker, close, and shake vigorously for about 20 seconds.

2 | Strain shaker contents into the collins glass over 3 ice cubes and serve with the straw.

➤ Non-alcoholic: To make a **Frothy Orange,** combine ⅛ cup plus 2 teaspoons blood orange juice, 4 teaspoons freshly squeezed lemon juice, 4 teaspoons grenadine, 1 egg white, and 4 ice cubes in a shaker, shake, and pour over ice.

Classic with a New Twist
Pisco Sour

MAKES 1 DRINK

➤ ¼ cup pisco

⅛ cup – ⅛ cup plus 2 tsp freshly squeezed lemon juice

1½ tbs sugar syrup (i.e. simple syrup)

1 fresh egg white

➤ Plus:

Ice cubes

Cocktail shaker

Bar strainer

Collins glass (8 oz)

1 straw

1 | Combine pisco, lemon juice, sugar syrup, egg white and 4 ice cubes in the shaker, close, and shake vigorously for about 20 seconds.

2 | Strain shaker contents into the collins glass over 3 ice cubes and serve with the straw.

➤ Non-alcoholic: To make a **Pineapple Sour,** combine ⅛ cup plus 2 teaspoons pineapple juice, 4 teaspoons freshly squeezed lemon juice, 2 teaspoons sugar syrup, and 3 ice cubes in a shaker, shake, and pour over ice. Garnish with 1 maraschino cherry.

Classic
Cosmopolitan

MAKES 1 DRINK

➤ ⅛ cup plus 2 tsp vodka
  1½ tbs orange liqueur
  (e.g. Cointreau)
  1½ tbs cranberry nectar
  1½ tbs freshly squeezed
  lime juice
➤ Plus:
  Ice cubes
  Cocktail shaker
  Bar strainer
  Martini glass (4 oz)

1 | Combine vodka, orange liqueur, cranberry nectar, lime juice, and 4 ice cubes in the shaker.

2 | Close shaker and shake vigorously for about 20 seconds. Strain shaker contents into the martini glass.

➤ Non-alcoholic: Combine 4 teaspoons cherry nectar, 4 teaspoons cranberry nectar, 4 teaspoons lime juice, and stir. Pour into a glass over 3 ice cubes and top up with ginger ale.

Bitter and Sour
Green Vamp

MAKES 1 DRINK

➤ 2 tsp absinthe (55% vol)
  1½ tbs blue curaçao
  ¼ cup orange juice
  1½ tbs freshly squeezed
  lemon juice
  1½ tbs Rose's Lime Juice
  2 tsp sugar syrup
  (i.e. simple syrup)
➤ For the garnish:
  1 orange slice
➤ Plus:
  Ice cubes
  Cocktail shaker
  Bar strainer
  Collins glass (8 oz)
  1 straw

1 | For the garnish, cut a slit halfway through an orange slice and place on the rim of the collins glass.

2 | Combine all the ingredients and 4 ice cubes in the shaker, close, and shake vigorously for about 20 seconds.

3 | Strain shaker contents into the prepared collins glass over an additional 3 ice cubes and serve with the straw.

Long Drink | Classic
Horse's Neck

MAKES 1 DRINK

➤ 1 piece lemon peel
  ⅛ cup plus 1 tbs bourbon
  1 dash Angostura
  Ice-cold ginger ale for
  topping up
➤ Plus:
  Ice cubes
  Collins glass (8 oz)
  1 straw

1 | Place 3 ice cubes and lemon peel in the collins glass. Pour on whiskey and Angostura.

2 | Top up with ginger ale. Stir once and serve with the straw.

TIP

To make this zesty drink more visually appealing, use a zester to grate off peel from a lemon. Or cut the piece of peel into long, thin strips.

Finely Tart | Fruity
Pisco Yellow

MAKES 1 DRINK

➤ ⅛ cup plus 2 tsp pisco

1½ tbs pineapple juice

1½ tbs grapefruit juice

1½ tbs Rose's Lime Juice

2 tsp sugar syrup
(i.e. simple syrup)

1 dash freshly squeezed
lemon juice

➤ Plus:

Ice cubes

Cocktail shaker

Bar strainer

Martini glass (4 oz)

1 straw

1 | Combine pisco, pineapple juice, grapefruit juice, lime juice, sugar syrup, lemon juice and 4 ice cubes in the shaker, close, and shake vigorously for about 20 seconds.

2 | Strain shaker contents into the collins glass over 3 ice cubes and serve with the straw.

➤ Non-alcoholic: Combine ⅛ cup plus 2 teaspoons orange juice, 4 teaspoons grapefruit juice, 4 teaspoons pineapple juice, 2 teaspoons lemon juice, and 3 ice cubes in a collins glass and stir. Top up with ginger ale.

Fresh | Bitter
Banana-Peppermint Liqueur

MAKES 1 DRINK

➤ 1½ tbs vodka

⅛ cup peppermint liqueur

⅛ cup banana liqueur

2 tsp freshly squeezed
lemon juice

Tonic water for topping up

1 dash Angostura

➤ For the garnish:

Mint sprig

➤ Plus:

Ice cubes

Cocktail shaker

Bar strainer

Collins glass (8 oz)

1 | Combine vodka, peppermint liqueur, banana liqueur, lemon juice and 4 ice cubes in the shaker, close, and shake vigorously for about 20 seconds.

2 | Strain shaker contents into the collins glass over 3 ice cubes. Top up with tonic water and add 1–2 dashes Angostura. Serve garnished with a mint sprig.

Mild | Fresh
Azzurino

MAKES 1 DRINK

➤ 2 tsp vodka

1½ tbs vermouth bianco
(e.g. Martini Bianco)

1½ tbs almond liqueur
(e.g. amaretto)

2 tsp blue curaçao

1½ tbs freshly squeezed
lemon juice

Lemon soda (e.g. 7up)
for topping up

➤ Plus:

Ice cubes

Cocktail shaker

Bar strainer

Collins glass (8 oz)

1 | Combine vodka, vermouth, amaretto, blue curaçao, lemon juice and 4 ice cubes in the shaker, close, and shake vigorously for about 20 seconds.

2 | Strain shaker contents into the collins glass over 3 ice cubes and top up with lemon soda.

Mildly Aromatic
Melissa

MAKES 1 DRINK

➤ 2 sprigs lemon balm
  1½ tbs cachaça
  1½ tbs freshly
  squeezed lemon
  ½ tsp sugar
  1 slice lemon
  Lemon soda (e.g. 7up)
  for topping up
  2 dashes raspberry syrup
➤ Plus:
  Crushed ice
  Muddler
  Rocks glass (5 oz)
  1 straw

1 | Rinse lemon balm and pinch off leaves. Place leaves, cachaça, lemon juice, and sugar in the rocks glass and crush slightly with the muddler.

2 | Place lemon slice in the glass and fill up with crushed ice. Pour on lemon soda, splash raspberry syrup on top, and serve with the straw.

Classic with a New Twist
Woodruff Julep

MAKES 1 DRINK

➤ 5–6 sprigs fresh woodruff
  (available in gourmet
  stores)
  ⅛ cup bourbon
  2 tsp sugar syrup
  (i.e. simple syrup)
  Ice-cold, dry sparkling
  wine for topping up
➤ Plus:
  Crushed ice
  Muddler
  Collins glass (8 oz)
  Straw

Standing time: 2 hours

1 | Place woodruff in the collins glass and crush slightly with the muddler. Pour on bourbon, cover, and let stand for 2 hours.

2 | Fill glass with crushed ice, pour on sugar syrup, and stir well. Top up with sparkling wine and serve with the straw.

Hemingway's Favorite
Mojito

MAKES 1 DRINK

➤ ⅛ cup plus 2 tsp freshly
  squeezed lime juice
  8–10 leaves fresh mint
  2 tsp sugar
  2 tsp sugar syrup
  (i.e. simple sugar)
  ¼ cup white rum
  1 dash club soda
➤ Plus:
  Crushed ice
  Muddler
  Rocks glass (5 oz)
  1 straw

1 | Combine lime juice, mint, sugar, and sugar syrup in the rocks glass. Crush mint slightly with the muddler. Pour on rum and fill up glass with crushed ice.

2 | Top up with club soda and stir once vigorously from top to bottom. Serve with the straw.

Herby and Spicy
Leprechaun

MAKES 1 DRINK

➤ 2 tsp passion fruit syrup
  $\frac{1}{4}$ cup pineapple juice
  $\frac{1}{8}$ cup plus 2 tsp green
  Chartreuse (herb liqueur)
  $1\frac{1}{2}$ tbs vermouth bianco
  (e.g. Martini Bianco)
  1 dash blue curaçao
➤ Plus:
  Ice cubes
  Cocktail shaker
  Bar strainer
  Rocks glass (5 oz)
  1 straw

1 | Combine passion fruit
syrup, pineapple juice,
Chartreuse, vermouth, and
4 ice cubes in the shaker.
Place top on shaker and
shake vigorously for about
20 seconds.

2 | Strain shaker contents into
the rocks glass, drizzle with
blue curaçao for decoration,
and serve with the straw.

Tart and Aromatic
Golden Grape

MAKES 1 DRINK

➤ 8 small seedless
  purple grapes
  $1\frac{1}{2}$ tbs cognac
  $\frac{1}{8}$ cup yellow Chartreuse
  (herb liqueur)
  $1\frac{1}{2}$ tbs white grape juice
  Club soda for topping up
➤ Plus:
  Ice cubes
  Cocktail shaker
  Bar strainer
  Collins glass (8 oz)

1 | Rinse grapes, cut in half,
and place in the collins glass
with 3 ice cubes.

2 | Combine cognac,
Chartreuse, lemon juice,
grape juice and 4 ice cubes
in the shaker, close, and
shake vigorously for about
20 seconds. Strain shaker
contents into the collins glass
and top up with club soda.

Tart and Sour
Abracadabra

MAKES 1 DRINK

➤ $1\frac{1}{2}$ tbs anisette
  (e.g. Ricard)
  $1\frac{1}{2}$ tbs brandy
  (e.g. Veterano)
  $1\frac{1}{2}$ tbs freshly squeezed
  lime juice
  $1\frac{1}{2}$ tbs sugar syrup
  (i.e. simple syrup)
➤ Plus:
  Ice cubes
  Cocktail shaker
  Bar strainer
  Martini glass (4 oz)

1 | Combine anisette, brandy,
lime juice, sugar syrup, and
4 ice cubes in the shaker.

2 | Close shaker and shake
vigorously for about 20 seconds. Strain shaker contents
into the martini glass.

Fresh & Fruity

Samba on the rocks and the Caribbean in a glass! That's what you get with cocktails containing lots of fruits and juices, preferably mixed with rum, cachaça, and tequila. They're just the right refreshment for hot summer nights.

Quick Recipes

Bellini

MAKES 1 DRINK

- ➤ ½ fresh, ripe peach
  1 dash grenadine syrup
  Ice-cold, dry sparkling wine
  for topping up
- ➤ Plus:
  Blender
  Champagne flute (2–3 oz)

1 | Rinse peach half, wipe dry, and peel carefully with a vegetable peeler. Cut into wedges.

2 | Combine peach pieces and grenadine in the blender and purée finely.

3 | Pour peach purée into the champagne flute and top up with sparkling wine.

Tequila Sunrise

MAKES 1 DRINK

- ➤ ¼ cup white tequila
  ½ cup orange juice
  2 tsp freshly squeezed lemon juice
  2–4 tsp grenadine syrup
- ➤ Plus:
  Ice cubes
  Large cocktail glass (10 oz)
  1 straw

1 | Place 4 ice cubes in the glass. Pour on tequila, orange juice and lemon juice, and stir once.

2 | Slowly drizzle grenadine over the drink. Carefully stir in a spiral direction from top to bottom. Serve with the straw.

Summery | Classic

Caipirinha

MAKES 1 DRINK

- 1 lime
  3 tsp brown sugar
  ¼ cup cachaça
- Plus:
  Crushed ice
  Muddler
  Rocks glass (5 oz)
  1 straw

1 | Rinse lime under hot water, wipe dry, cut into quarters, and cut quarters in half. Place in the rocks glass and sprinkle with sugar. Crush limes thoroughly with the muddler.

2 | Fill rocks glass with crushed ice and pour on cachaça. Give it one good stir and serve with the straw.

- Non-alcoholic: Crush the lime with sugar as described. Add ¼ cup passion fruit nectar. Fill rocks glass with crushed ice and top up with club soda. Stir well.

Fresh | Exotic

Kumpirinha

MAKES 1 DRINK

- 5 kumquats
  1 tsp brown sugar
  ⅛ cup plus 2 tsp gin
  1½ tbs vermouth bianco
  (e.g. Martini Bianco)
  1 tsp orange liqueur
  (e.g. Cointreau)
- Plus:
  Crushed ice
  Muddler
  Rocks glass (5 oz)
  1 straw

1 | Rinse kumquats under hot water, wipe dry, and slice finely, removing the seeds. Place the slices in the rocks glass, sprinkle with sugar, and crush slightly with the muddler.

2 | Fill rocks glass with crushed ice and pour on remaining ingredients. Give it one good stir. Cut straw in half and serve with the straws.

Fruity and Sour

Pomme de Cassis

MAKES 1 DRINK

- ½ lime
  2 tsp sugar syrup
  (i.e. simple syrup)
  5 leaves fresh mint
  ⅛ cup plus 2 tsp vodka
  1½ tbs crème de cassis
  (black currant liqueur)
  Unfiltered apple juice for
  topping up
- Plus:
  Crushed ice
  Muddler
  Large cocktail glass (10 oz)
  1 straw

1 | Rinse lime under hot water, wipe dry, cut into 12 pieces, and place in the cocktail glass along with sugar syrup. Squeeze out limes thoroughly with the muddler. Rinse mint leaves, pat dry, add, and crush.

2 | Fill glass half full with crushed ice. Add vodka, then cassis. Top up with apple juice, stir briefly, and serve with the straw.

Strong | Classic
Mai Tai

MAKES 1 DRINK

➤ ½ lime

⅛ cup plus 1 tbs dark rum

1½ tbs orange liqueur (e.g. Cointreau)

2 tsp freshly squeezed lime juice

2 tsp sugar syrup (i.e. simple syrup)

2 tsp almond syrup (orgeat)

➤ Plus:

Crushed ice

Ice cubes

Cocktail shaker

Bar strainer

Collins glass (8 oz)

2 straws

1 | Fill collins glass half full with crushed ice. Cut lime half into quarters and squeeze over the glass. Then drop lime pieces into the glass.

2 | Combine remaining ingredients and 4 ice cubes in the shaker, close, and shake vigorously for about 20 seconds. Strain shaker contents into the glass and stir briefly. Serve with the straws.

High-Proof
Zombie

MAKES 1 DRINK

➤ 1½ tbs dark rum

1½ tbs white rum

2 tsp rum (73 proof)

1½ tbs cherry brandy

⅓ cup mango nectar

⅛ cup cherry nectar

1½ tbs blood orange juice

1½ tbs lemon juice

1 dash cherry syrup

➤ Plus:

Ice cubes

Cocktail shaker

Bar strainer

Large cocktail glass (10 oz)

1 straw

1 | Combine 3 types of rum, brandy, mango nectar, cherry nectar, blood orange juice, lemon juice, cherry syrup, and 4 ice cubes in the shaker.

2 | Close shaker and shake vigorously for about 20 seconds. Strain contents into the glass over 3–4 ice cubes and serve with the straw.

Classic with a New Twist
Planter's New Punch

MAKES 1 DRINK

➤ ¼ cup dark rum

⅛ cup plus 2 tsp pineapple juice

1½ tbs orange juice

1½ tbs grapefruit juice

2–2½ tsp sugar syrup (i.e. simple sugar)

⅛ cup club soda

➤ Plus:

Ice cubes

Cocktail shaker

Bar strainer

Large cocktail glass (10 oz)

1 straw

1 | Combine rum, juices, sugar syrup and 4 ice cubes in the shaker, close, and shake vigorously for about 20 seconds.

2 | Strain shaker contents into the cocktail glass over 3 ice cubes. Top up with club soda and serve with the straw.

Classic with a New Twist

Capt'n Blueberry

MAKES 1 DRINK

➤ ¼ cup thawed, frozen blueberries

¼ cup plus 2 tsp white rum

⅛ cup freshly squeezed lime juice

2½ tsp sugar syrup (i.e. simple syrup)

➤ Plus:

Crushed ice

Blender

Collins glass (8 oz)

1 straw

1 │ In a blender, combine blueberries, rum, lime juice, sugar syrup, and 5 tablespoons crushed ice.

2 │ Blend until the blueberries are completely puréed. Pour into the collins glass and serve with the straw.

➤ Traditional: Without the blueberries, the Capt'n Blueberry becomes a **Daiquiri**: Combine ⅛ cup plus 1 tablespoon white rum, 4 teaspoons freshly squeezed lime juice, 2 teaspoons sugar syrup and 4 ice cubes in a shaker, shake vigorously for about 20 seconds, and strain into a martini glass (4 oz).

Fruity and Aromatic

Autumn Cobbler

MAKES 1 DRINK

➤ 3 small plums

1½ tbs bourbon

2½ tsp sugar syrup (i.e. simple syrup)

1 dash freshly squeezed lemon juice

⅛ cup plus 2 tsp red grape juice

Dry red wine for topping up

➤ Plus:

Crushed ice

Collins glass (8 oz)

1 straw

1 long-handled spoon

1 │ Rinse plums, wipe dry, cut in half, remove pits, and dice finely. Place in the collins glass.

2 │ Pour bourbon, sugar syrup and lemon juice over the plums, and stir well.

3 │ Fill the glass with crushed ice to within about ¾ inch of the top. Add grape juice and top up with red wine. Give it one good stir and serve with the straw and spoon.

Tartly Tropical

Desert Island

MAKES 1 DRINK

➤ 1½ tbs white tequila

1½ tbs cachaça

2 tsp crème de bananes

⅛ cup orange juice

⅛ cup pineapple juice

1½ tbs freshly squeezed lime juice

1½ tbs sugar syrup (i.e. simple syrup)

➤ Plus:

Ice cubes

Cocktail shaker

Collins glass (8 oz)

1 straw

1 │ Combine tequila, cachaça, crème de bananes, orange juice, pineapple juice, lime juice, sugar syrup and 4 ice cubes in the shaker, close, and shake vigorously for about 20 seconds.

2 │ Strain shaker contents into the collins glass over 3 ice cubes and serve with the straw.

Fresh and Fruity
Red Melon

MAKES 1 DRINK

➤ ¼ lb watermelon
  ⅛ cup Campari
  ⅛ cup vermouth bianco
  (e.g. Martini Bianco)
  1½ tbs melon liqueur
  1 dash grenadine syrup
➤ Plus:
  Ice cubes
  Blender
  Collins glass (8 oz)

1 | Remove seeds from melon and cut up coarsely. In the blender, purée melon with Campari, vermouth, melon liqueur, grenadine, and 3 ice cubes.

2 | Pour into the glass over 3 ice cubes.

➤ Non-alcoholic: Cut up ⅛ lb (¼ cup) cantaloupe and cleaned strawberries and purée in a blender with ⅓ cup plus 1½ tablespoons orange juice, 2 teaspoons freshly squeezed lime juice, and 1 dash grenadine. Pour into a glass and top up with lemon soda (e.g. 7up).

Fruity and Aromatic
Cherry Mint Julep

MAKES 1 DRINK

➤ 10–15 leaves fresh mint
  1 tsp sugar syrup
  (i.e. simple syrup)
  ¼ cup cherry brandy
  1½ tbs cherry nectar
  Club soda for topping up
➤ Plus:
  Crushed ice
  Muddler
  Collins glass (8 oz)
  1 straw

1 | Rinse mint under cold water, pat dry, and place in the collins glass. Add sugar syrup and 2 tablespoons club soda. Crush mint slightly with the muddler.

2 | Fill glass half full with crushed ice. First add cherry brandy and then cherry nectar. Top up with mineral water, stir briefly, and serve with the straw.

Refreshing
Floridita

MAKES 1 DRINK

➤ ⅛ lb fresh pineapple
  (peeled)
  2 tsp Rose's Lime Juice
  ⅛ cup white rum
  2 tsp orange liqueur
  (e.g. Cointreau)
  2 tsp sugar syrup
  (i.e. simple syrup)
  1 scoop lemon sorbet
  (from the supermarket)
➤ Plus:
  Ice cubes
  Blender
  Large cocktail glass (10 oz)
  1 straw

1 | Clean pineapple and cut into small pieces. In the blender, combine lime juice, rum, orange liqueur, sugar syrup, and 3 ice cubes. Blend until the ice cubes and pineapple are reduced to slush.

2 | Add lemon sorbet and blend briefly. Pour into the cocktail glass and serve with the straw.

Fruity and Sweet
Strawberry Blonde

MAKES 1 DRINK

➤ $1/4$ cup fresh or thawed, frozen strawberries (3–4 berries)

$1/8$ cup plus 2 tsp white rum

$1/3$ cup plus $1\frac{1}{2}$ tbs pineapple juice

$1\frac{1}{2}$ tbs strawberry syrup

➤ Plus:

Ice cubes

Blender

Large cocktail glass (10 oz)

1 straw

1 | Rinse fresh strawberries, clean and chop, or leave thawed frozen berries whole. Place in the blender with rum, pineapple juice, strawberry syrup, and 3 ice cubes. Blend until the ice cubes are reduced to slush.

2 | Pour strawberry-rum mixture into the cocktail glass over 3 ice cubes and serve with the straw.

Short Drink
Margarita

MAKES 1 DRINK

➤ $1/8$ cup pus 2 tsp white tequila

$1\frac{1}{2}$ tbs orange liqueur (e.g. Cointreau)

$1\frac{1}{2}$ tbs freshly squeezed lemon juice

➤ For the garnish:

$1/2$ lemon

Salt (sprinkled onto a plate)

➤ Plus:

Ice cubes

Cocktail shaker

Bar strainer

Martini glass (4 oz)

1 | Rub rim of martini glass with the lemon quarter and dip into the salt. Gently knock off excess salt.

2 | Combine tequila, orange liqueur, lemon juice and 4 ice cubes in the shaker, close, and shake vigorously for about 20 seconds.

3 | Strain shaker contents into the martini glass.

Party Drink
Kiwi Limes

MAKES 1 DRINK

➤ 1 piece peeled kiwi ($1/8$ lb)

$1/8$ cup plus 1 tbs vodka

$1/8$ cup plus 1 tbs dry sparkling wine

$1\frac{1}{2}$ tbs Rose's Lime Juice

$2\frac{1}{2}$ tsp sugar syrup (i.e. simply syrup)

➤ Plus:

Crushed ice

Blender

Large cocktail glass (10 oz)

1 straw

1 | Finely chop kiwi and place in the blender with vodka, sparkling wine, lime juice, sugar syrup, and 5 tablespoons crushed ice.

2 | Mix until the kiwi is completely puréed, pour into the cocktail glass, and serve with the straw.

➤ Variation: To make **Strawberry Limes,** use $1/4$ cup (or 7 small strawberries) fresh or thawed frozen strawberries.

Mild | Light
Pink Cloud

MAKES 1 DRINK

➤ 5 small strawberries
⅛ plus 2 tsp white rum
⅛ cup vermouth bianco
(e.g. Martini Bianco)
1½ tbs melon liqueur
2 dashes strawberry syrup
Club soda for topping up
➤ Plus:
Ice cubes
Cocktail shaker
Bar strainer
Collins glass (8 oz)

1 | Rinse strawberries, clean, gently pat dry, and cut into quarters.

2 | Combine rum, vermouth, melon liqueur, strawberry syrup and 4 ice cubes in the shaker, close, and shake vigorously for about 20 seconds.

3 | Place 3 ice cubes and strawberries in the glass. Strain shaker contents over the top, top up with mineral water, and serve immediately.

Fruity and Sweet
Ginello

MAKES 1 DRINK

➤ ⅛ cup plus 2 tsp gin
1½ tbs peach liqueur
1½ tbs apricot brandy
¼ cup freshly squeezed pink grapefruit juice
¼ cup mango nectar
2 tsp almond syrup (orgeat)
➤ Plus:
Ice cubes
Cocktail shaker
Bar strainer
Collins glass (8 oz)
1 straw

1 | Combine gin, peach liqueur, apricot brandy, grapefruit juice, mango nectar, almond syrup, and 4 ice cubes in the shaker.

2 | Close shaker and shake vigorously for about 20 seconds. Strain shaker contents into the collins glass over 3–4 ice cubes and serve with the straw.

Refreshing
Chapple Shake

MAKES 1 DRINK

➤ ⅛ cup plus 2 tsp white rum
1½ tbs cherry brandy
¼ cup unfiltered apple juice
⅛ cup plus 2 tsp cherry nectar
➤ Plus:
Ice cubes
Cocktail shaker
Bar strainer
Collins glass (8 oz)
1 straw

1 | Combine rum, cherry brandy, apple juice, cherry nectar and 4 ice cubes in the shaker, close, and shake vigorously for about 20 seconds.

2 | Pour shaker contents into the collins glass over 3 ice cubes and serve with the straw.

Smooth & Creamy

Melting in your mouth, heavenly sweet, and diabolically delicious, even the strongest spirits seem harmless when they're wrapped in cream, coconut milk, or crème liqueur. So be careful! You don't need to have a sweet tooth to find yourself wanting more.

Quick Recipes

White Cloud

MAKES 1 DRINK

➤ ⅛ cup plus 2 tsp vodka
   1½ tbs white crème de cacao
   ¼ cup pineapple juice
   1½ tbs cream

➤ Plus:
   Ice cubes | Crushed ice
   Cocktail shaker
   Bar strainer
   Collins glass (8 oz)
   1 straw

1 | Combine vodka, crème de cacao, pineapple juice, cream and 4 ice cubes in the shaker, close, and shake vigorously for about 20 seconds.

2 | Fill collins glass about one-third full with crushed ice. Strain shaker contents over the ice and serve with the straw.

Grasshopper

MAKES 1 DRINK

➤ 1½ tbs white crème de cacao
   1½ tbs green crème de menthe
   ⅛ cup plus 2 tsp cream

➤ Plus:
   Ice cubes | Cocktail shaker
   Bar strainer | Martini glass (4 oz)

1 | Combine crème de cacao, crème de menthe, cream and 4 ice cubes in the shaker, close, and shake vigorously for about 20 seconds. Strain shaker contents into the martini glass.

Tip: There are many different recipes for this cream cocktail. Try them out and see which ones taste best. For example, here's a drink that requires a 5 ounce martini glass: Combine ⅛ cup white crème de cacao, ⅛ cup green crème de menthe and ⅛ cup plus 2 teaspoons cream, and shake as described above.

47

Digestif | Fruity
Casanova

MAKES 1 DRINK

- ➤ 2½ tsp Calvados
  1 tsp orange liqueur
  (e.g. Cointreau)
  ⅛ cup plus 2 tsp
  orange juice
  2 tsp cream
  1 tsp sugar syrup
  (i.e. simply syrup)
- ➤ For the garnish:
  1 spiral piece of
  orange peel
- ➤ Plus:
  Ice cubes
  Cocktail shaker
  Bar strainer
  Martini glass (4 oz)

1 | Combine Calvados, orange liqueur, orange juice, cream, sugar syrup and 4 ice cubes in the shaker, close, and shake vigorously for about 20 seconds.

2 | Strain shaker contents into the martini glass. Hang orange peel on the rim and serve immediately.

Classic and Tropical
Swimming Pool

MAKES 1 DRINK

- ➤ ⅛ cup white rum
  1½ tbs vodka
  ⅓ cup plus 1½ tbs
  pineapple juice
  1½ tbs cream
  2 tsp cream of coconut
  (canned)
  2 tsp blue curaçao
- ➤ Plus:
  Crushed ice
  Blender
  Large cocktail glass (10 oz)

1 | In the blender, blend rum, vodka, pineapple juice, cream, and cream of coconut until well mixed and foamy.

2 | Fill cocktail glass half full with crushed ice. Pour mixture over the top and give it a good stir. Drizzle blue curaçao over the finished cocktail.

Digestif
Golden Cadillac

MAKES 1 DRINK

- ➤ 1½ tbs white crème
  de cacao
  2 tsp Galliano
  ⅛ cup plus 2 tsp
  orange juice
  1½ tbs cream
- ➤ Plus:
  Ice cubes
  Cocktail shaker
  Bar strainer
  Martini glass (4 oz)

1 | Combine crème de cacao, Galliano, orange juice, cream and 4 ice cubes in the shaker, close, and shake vigorously for about 20 seconds.

2 | Strain shaker contents into the martini glass.

Summery | Mild

Toscanello

MAKES 1 DRINK

- ½ ripe peach
  2 tsp bourbon
  2 tsp almond liqueur
  (e.g. amaretto)
  1½ tbs cream
  1 dash grenadine syrup
- For the garnish:
  1 peach wedge
- Plus:
  Ice cubes
  Blender
  Martini glass (4 oz)

1 | Rinse half peach, pat dry, remove pit, and chop finely. In the blender, combine peach with bourbon, almond liqueur, cream, grenadine, and 3 ice cubes. Blend until the ice cubes and peach are reduced to slush.

2 | Pour into the martini glass and garnish the rim with the peach wedge.

Wintry Digestif

Dream of Cream

MAKES 1 DRINK

- 1½ tbs almond liqueur
  (e.g. amaretto)
  1½ tbs unfiltered
  apple juice
  2 tsp cream
  1 tsp vanilla syrup
- For the garnish:
  ½ lemon
  Ground almonds
- Plus:
  Ice cubes
  Cocktail shaker
  Bar strainer
  Martini glass (4 oz)

1 | For the garnish, rub the rim of the glass with the lemon quarter and dip into the ground almonds.

2 | Combine almond liqueur, apple juice, cream, vanilla syrup and 4 ice cubes in the shaker, close, and shake vigorously for about 20 seconds.

3 | Strain shaker contents into the prepared martini glass and serve immediately.

Digestif | Fruity

Irish Summer Sun

MAKES 1 DRINK

- 1½ tbs Irish cream
  (e.g. Bailey's)
  1½ tbs coconut liqueur
  ⅛ cup orange juice
  2 tsp cream
- Plus:
  Ice cubes
  Cocktail shaker
  Bar strainer
  Martini glass (4 oz)

1 | Combine Irish cream, coconut liqueur, orange juice, cream and 4 ice cubes in the shaker, close, and shake vigorously for about 20 seconds.

2 | Strain shaker contents into the martini glass and serve immediately.

Creamy and Fruity
Melba Rumba

MAKES 1 DRINK

➤ ½ cup raspberries
⅛ cup dark rum
⅛ cup orange liqueur (e.g. Cointreau)
⅛ cup cream
½ cup peach nectar
➤ Plus:
Ice cubes
Blender
Cocktail shaker
Bar strainer
Collins glass (8 oz)
1 straw

1 | Rinse raspberries, clean, purée finely, and place in the collins glass.

2 | Combine rum, orange liqueur, cream, peach nectar and 4 ice cubes in the shaker, close, and shake vigorously for about 20 seconds. Carefully strain shaker contents onto the raspberry purée.

3 | Using the straw, carefully stir the raspberry in a spiral direction from bottom to top and serve.

Mild
Sun Ray

MAKES 1 DRINK

➤ 2 large, ripe apricots
⅛ cup Galliano
⅛ cup white rum
1½ tbs orange liqueur (e.g. Cointreau)
⅛ cup cream
⅓ cup peach nectar
2 tsp grenadine syrup
➤ Plus:
Ice cubes
Blender
Cocktail shaker
Bar strainer
Collins glass (8 oz)

1 | Rinse apricots, cut into quarters, remove pits, and purée finely in the blender.

2 | Combine puréed apricots, Galliano, rum, orange liqueur, cream, peach nectar and 4 ice cubes in the shaker, close, and shake vigorously for about 20 seconds.

3 | Strain shaker contents into the collins glass over 3 ice cubes. Drizzle grenadine down the inside of the glass in four places to make decorative stripes.

Classic with a New Twist
Mango Colada

MAKES 1 DRINK

➤ 1 piece peeled mango (⅛ cup)
⅛ cup white rum
2 tsp passion fruit nectar
1½ tbs mango nectar
⅛ cup unsweetened coconut milk (canned)
2½ tsp vanilla syrup
➤ Plus:
Crushed ice
Blender
Collins glass (8 oz)
1 straw

1 | Combine mango, rum, passion fruit nectar, mango nectar and vanilla syrup in the blender, and mix until the mango is completely puréed.

2 | Fill collins glass one-third full with crushed ice. Pour blender contents over the top and serve with the straw.

Creamy | Refreshing
Bella Russia

MAKES 1 DRINK

➤ ½ cup vanilla ice cream
⅛ cup plus 2 tsp vodka
2 tsp Galliano
Club soda for topping up
2–2½ tsp strawberry syrup

➤ For the garnish:
1 fresh strawberry with
the stem

➤ Plus:
Crushed ice
Blender
Large cocktail glass (10 oz)
1 straw

1 | Slit strawberry halfway
through and place it on the
rim of the cocktail glass.

2 | Fill large cocktail glass
about one-third full with
crushed ice.

3 | In the blender, mix ice
cream, vodka, and Galliano.
Pour blender contents over
the crushed ice.

4 | Top up with club soda and
stir briefly. Carefully drizzle
strawberry syrup into the
finished drink and serve with
the straw.

Aromatic and Sweet
Choc-Choc

MAKES 1 DRINK

➤ ⅛ cup chocolate ice cream
⅛ cup plus 2 tsp brandy
(e.g. Veterano)
1½ tbs crème de cassis
(blank currant liqueur)
½ cup red grape juice

➤ Plus:
Crushed ice
Blender
Large cocktail glass (10 oz)
1 straw

1 | In the blender, combine
chocolate ice cream, brandy,
crème de cassis, grape juice,
and 3 tablespoons crushed
ice and blend.

2 | Blend until you have a
smooth liquid. Pour into the
cocktail glass and serve with
the straw.

Creamy | Aromatic
Bourbon Vanilla Soda

MAKES 1 DRINK

➤ ½ cup vanilla ice cream
⅛ cup bourbon
1½ tbs vanilla syrup
Club soda for topping up

➤ Plus:
Blender
Ice cubes
Collins glass (8 oz)
1 straw

1 | In the blender, mix vanilla
ice cream, bourbon, and
vanilla syrup until you have
a smooth liquid.

2 | Pour blender contents into
the collins glass over 3 ice
cubes, top up with club soda,
and serve with the straw.

Hot and Fruity
Hot Vodka Melon

MAKES 1 DRINK

➤ ⅛ lb cantaloupe
½ tsp fresh peeled ginger
½ cup vodka
1½ tbs orange juice
⅛ cup buttermilk
2½ tsp sugar syrup
(i.e. simply syrup)
➤ Plus:
Ice cubes
Blender
Large cocktail glass (10 oz)
1 straw

1 │ Chop melon and dice ginger very finely. In the blender, purée melon, ginger, and vodka.

2 │ Add orange juice, buttermilk, sugar syrup, and 3–4 ice cubes and mix until the ice cubes are reduced to slush.

3 │ Pour blender contents into the cocktail glass over 3 ice cubes and serve with the straw.

Caribbean / Mild
Banana Boat

MAKES 1 DRINK

➤ ½ ripe banana
⅛ cup plus 2 tsp white rum
1½ tbs Galliano
1½ tbs passion fruit syrup
½ cup pineapple juice
½ cup unsweetened coconut milk (canned)
1½ tbs cream
➤ Plus:
Ice cubes
Blender
Large cocktail glass (10 oz)
1 straw

1 │ Peel banana and chop coarsely. In the blender, combine banana, rum, Galliano, passion fruit syrup, pineapple juice, coconut milk, cream and 3 ice cubes, and mix until the ice cubes reduce to slush.

2 │ Pour blender contents into the cocktail glass over 3 ice cubes and serve with the straw.

Creamy and Mild
Amalfino

MAKES 1 DRINK

➤ 1½ tbs blue curaçao
1½ tbs almond liqueur (e.g. amaretto)
⅛ cup plus 2 tsp orange juice
1½ tbs cream
➤ Plus:
Ice cubes
Cocktail shaker
Bar strainer
Martini glass (4 oz)

1 │ Combine curaçao, almond liqueur, orange juice, cream, and 4 ice cubes in the shaker.

2 │ Close the shaker and shake vigorously for about 20 seconds. Strain shaker contents into the martini glass.

➤ Non-alcoholic: Shake 1½ tablespoons blue curaçao, ⅛ cup plus 1 tablespoon banana nectar, ⅛ cup plus 1 tablespoon orange juice, ⅛ cup plus 1 tablespoon buttermilk and 4 ice cubes, and pour into a martini glass (4 oz).

Classic | Digestif
Brandy Alexander

MAKES 1 DRINK

- ⅛ cup plus 2 tsp brandy (e.g. Veterano)

  ⅛ cup dark crème de cacao

  1½ tbs cream

  2 tbs whipped cream

  1 pinch freshly grated nutmeg
- Plus:

  Ice cubes

  Cocktail shaker

  Bar strainer

  Martini glass (4 oz)

1 | Combine brandy, crème de cacao, liquid and whipped creams, and 4 ice cubes in the shaker, close, and shake vigorously for about 20 seconds.

2 | Strain shaker contents into the martini glass and sprinkle with nutmeg.

- Non-alcoholic: Shake 1½ tablespoons cream of coconut, 1½ tablespoons chocolate syrup, ⅛ cup cream, ⅛ cup plus 1 tablespoon milk and 4 ice cubes, and pour into a martini glass.

Invigorating Digestif
Banana Coffee

MAKES 1 DRINK

- 2 tsp vodka

  2 tsp coffee liqueur

  ⅛ cup banana nectar

  2 tsp cream

  1 tsp vanilla syrup
- For the garnish:

  3 small banana slices

  A little lemon juice

  1 yellow cocktail skewer
- Plus:

  Ice cubes

  Cocktail shaker

  Bar strainer

  Martini glass (4 oz)

1 | For the garnish, drizzle banana slices with lemon juice, thread onto the cocktail skewer, and set aside.

2 | Combine vodka, coffee liqueur, banana nectar, cream, vanilla syrup and 4 ice cubes in the shaker, and shake vigorously for about 20 seconds.

3 | Strain shaker contents into the martini glass, place cocktail skewer across the rim, and serve.

Creamy and Bitter
Friar's Coffee

MAKES 1 DRINK

- 1 tsp instant espresso powder

  1½ tbs brandy

  1½ tbs hazelnut liqueur (e.g. Frangelico)

  2 tsp white crème de cacao

  2 tsp coffee liqueur

  ⅛ cup plus 1 tbs cream

  Cocoa powder for sprinkling
- Plus:

  Ice cubes

  Cocktail shaker

  Bar strainer

  Martini glass (4 oz)

1 | Dissolve espresso powder in 1 tablespoon hot water. Combine espresso, brandy, hazelnut liqueur, crème de cacao, coffee liqueur, cream and 4 ice cubes in the shaker, close, and shake vigorously for about 20 seconds.

2 | Strain shaker contents into the martini glass and dust with cocoa powder.

The Authors

Alessandra Redies and Tanja Dusy share a mutual passion for mixing, stirring, and shaking. They've already produced three successful books entitled *Cocktails*, *Winter Drinks*, and *Coffee and Espresso*. But developing lively drinks isn't their only job; the two also work as cookbook editors for European publishers.

The Photographer

Kai Mewes is an independent food photographer in Germany who works for publishers and in advertising. His appetizing photos reflect his dedication to combining digital photography, styling, and culinary pleasure. In this book, food styling is the work of Daniel Petri.

Photo Credits

Cover photo: Michael Brauner, Karsruhe
All others: Kai Mewes

Published originally under the title *Cocktails & Drinks: klassisch und trendig* © 2004 Gräfe und Unzer Verlag GmbH, Munich. English translation for the U.S. market © 2006, Silverback Books, Inc.

Program director: Doris Birk
Managing editor: Birgit Rademacker
Editors: Stefanie Poziombka, Susanne Klug, Lisa M. Tooker (US)
Translator: Christie Tam (US)
Proofreader: Susanne Klug
Typesetting: Verlagssatz Lingner
Layout, typography and cover design: Independent Medien Design, Munich
Production: Gloria Pall, Patty Holden (US)

Printed in China

ISBN: 1-59637-102-1

Enjoy Other Quick & Easy Books

Mushrooms

Cornelia Schinharl

Cooking for One

Christian Kompe

Bread Machine

Ellen A. Hatch

Cooking for Children

V. Cramm

Preserves and Canning

Irresistible Fondue

Angelika Illies

Cooking for Two

Cornelia Adam

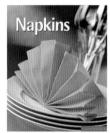

Napkins

Fast Italian

Margit Proebst

Andreas Furtmayr

Sushi

Classic ideas from Japan and new fusion sushi
Home-made perfectly

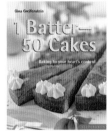

Gina Greifenstein

1 Batter—50 Cakes

Baking to your heart's content

Cooking in Clay

Healthy Recipes with Great Flavor

Erika Casparek-Türkkan

Coffee and Espresso

Tanja Dusy

Grilling

Crisp, flavorful veggies—vegetable sprouts from the grill for that robust food, from spareribs to skewered veggies, with sauces and chutneys.

Sauces and Dips

Soups

Classic to Contemporary

Sebastian Dickhaut

Claudia Schmidt

Raclette

New Recipes with Cheese Fondue and Party Dips

Antipasti and Tapas

Mediterranean Appetizers

Cornelia Schinharl

1 Pan—50 Muffins

Cornelia Adam

Salads

An array of standards, first appetizers/entrées, and party dishes. Includes ethnic choices and cutting-edge alternatives.

Sandwiches

Xenia Burgtorf

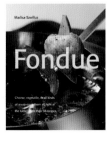

Marlisa Szwillus

Fondue

Cheese, vegetable, & all kinds of meat—choose from all night of the table, with from 50 recipes

Christmas Cookies

BAR UTENSILS

➤ You must have: Jigger, cocktail shaker, a bar strainer if needed, ice cube trays or a bag of ice, and a blender.

➤ Nice to have: Ice crusher, muddler, mixing glass, and bar spoon.

Guaranteed Perfect Cocktails & Mixed Drinks

SPIRITS

➤ Be sure to use quality spirits: A cocktail is only as good as its ingredients. Avoid bargains that seem too cheap to be true.

➤ Don't put too many different spirits into one cocktail—less is usually more.

➤ Select harmonious combinations (see pages 8–10).

SHAKING

➤ Make sure the shaker is well sealed so it won't leak.

➤ Shake the shaker up and down vigorously for about 20 seconds until condensation forms on the outside. Then pour the drink into the glass immediately so the ice won't water it down.

STIRRING

➤ Place the ingredients and 8–10 ice cubes in the mixing glass or in the bottom part of the shaker and stir vigorously with a bar spoon (or the handle of a mixing spoon) for 6–10 seconds. Strain through the bar strainer over 3 additional ice cubes, if desired.